Learning
to be Very Soft

Callan Waldron-Hall

smith|doorstop

Published 2020 by Smith|Doorstop Books
The Poetry Business
Campo House,
54 Campo Lane,
Sheffield S1 2EG
www.poetrybusiness.co.uk

ISBN 978-1-912196-29-6
Designed & Typeset by Utter
Printed by Biddles

Smith|Doorstop books are a member of Inpress: www.inpressbooks.co.uk.
Distributed by NBN International, 1 Deltic Avenue, Rooksley, Milton Keynes,
MK13 8LD.

The Poetry Business gratefully acknowledges the support of
Arts Council England.

Contents

For Mom and Dad

Chest Compressions

by the pool again one boy is pretending
he isn't breathing / that his heart has stopped
so his friend leans down / exhales

what he believes is life into
the wet cave of the other's mouth
then linking his fingers / simulates

a steady heartbeat / but not so much
as to crack the ribs / imagines his friend
coughing out water / the way he'd shudder

and when they are both dry / neither will
think of the past hour as practice /
how oddly rehearsed and familiar

until perhaps years later / in his room
one boy will remember / how he lay
in precise stillness / inches from

the edge of the pool / holding
his breath / not daring to move /
not daring to break character

Sister arrives after the floods

Sister has come to stay for the week. She says the floods in her town got too bad, found their way inside her house and ruined her favourite sofa. Sister says next time she will remember to draw her curtains more tightly. She says she has never seen rain come down the way it did against her roof, that there was so much she had to leave behind: her best comb, her sharpest scissors. Sister says without her scissors, how will she ever be productive again? As soon as she arrives she heads to my kitchen and turns on the cold tap, says the water here is nothing like the riverstreet at home. She tells me to watch as the sink fills up and spills over the lip, drenching her shoes. Sister says even here the water can reach her – it always will – yet look how easy she can make it stop.

Careful

After Karen Solie

to be careful is the condition of sisters   for the tucked-in
bedsheets and loose hairs   Sister   your room is made
from parts of me   and in places   the piling of our clothes
in heaps   our mother who moves through mountains of girl
is ground-breaking   a pioneer among those avoiding
hard work   you will not be remembered for leaving the house
and stepping into a new life   you must be accepting of this
though you wouldn't think twice about sleeping on sofas
and if you can name one person who cares for you
who is not quite a sister then –

imagine yourself being missed   you may have to dig out
the skirts you took from me   when your own clothes stay
so new   your new house so clean   still ruin everything
you can   no one will tidy   Sister your moving out is
like a landslide   you are devastating   tied to so little
your absence   I've been struggling to stand

Bragging Rights

Half-dozing in the back seat, I listen
to the silent concentration of Mom
carefully working the pedals of the car,

pulsing the accelerator as if frightened
she might urge us down the road too fast,
panic Dad sitting beside her, already

uncomfortable in the passenger seat.
He drives for a living, knows every junction
in the Midlands. But we are somewhere south

returning home from a caravan holiday
at night. Everything is disturbingly louder
when I am almost asleep. I can hear

Dad coolly memorising the way
the road slopes, Mom's hands tensing
the wheel, the gears clunking, Dad's words

sprawling the space between them.
They've been arguing, of course –
something about Mom not being able to,

or scared, or regretful. She hasn't said
a word since, just listened, like me, hoping
how perhaps next month she might quietly

enter the room holding two learning plates
behind her back, how they might sigh when
she tosses them, their soft weight falling.

I Could Never Save Someone on a Full Stomach

It's been debunked now so I'm feeling less guilty

It turns out I would have had no problem saving you
that Thursday when I used to eat and eat

'Saving' is rich isn't it? You taught people how
to swim for a living

All those swimmers and me watching bloated

Any other day and I could have held the entire pool
in the dip between my ribs and hips

So many people learn how to swim but not enough
learn how to not drown

Mom used to cook me pasta before swimming
because I grew up believing it was dangerous
to eat heavy food before you swam

How many grams of pasta can you eat
before it's considered heavy?

I suppose it's a good job it happened when it did

When I wasn't there I mean

I wouldn't have been helpful at all in fact
I would have just stood there watching it happen
saying I'm sorry I've eaten so much I can't help

Halocline

I

Sister I've been swimming now
for as long as I remember
thinking we are nearly
there but something
isn't quite right my lungs
are burning the surface seems
so far so alien a distant shore
so close   so close

II

Sister you are stirring salt
into a glass of water telling me
to watch when it settles
you are slowly pouring freshwater
on top look you say look
at how similar they seem
how they refuse to mix

III

Sister you are comforting me
a day later when the bruising
on my ribs finally darkens
it looks just like the water
doesn't it you tell me
to be untrusting of bruises
they change their faces appear
more terrible than they seem
you say they are villains
we must touch them to be sure

Brake

It was me

I was the one throwing stones
at the last train home that Tuesday

I was aiming at the driver's head

I have remarkably good aim

If I'd known how to drive a train then I would have
stopped the entire thing

I think I remember someone telling me once
about emergency brakes

The trains we ride only have alarms

We can only suggest stopping

If someone is having a medical emergency it is best to wait
until the train arrives at the next station

Do you think never wanting to leave counts?

I think the stone that hit was a suggestion

And the train
well it went straight through

Problem Pie

Sister says imagine the problem with double glazing –

What if it isn't installed correctly! Water
might creep between the panes and ruin
the illusion that there's nothing between her

and the outside. Imagine the place she visits
has no windows, of course this is only how
you think of it, though plenty of walls, plenty

pretending to be glass, to be transparent.
Though, she says, you're lucky you struggle
imagining it. The doctor tells her to view

everything like a pie. Every week he asks
about her Problem Pie – how will we manage
the portions, how will we cut everything up?

Imagine her adding to her list of banned verbs,
finding out including too much filling in the mix
prevents her pie from cooking right through.

Imagine her seeing you less and less. Something
about condensation. Something about ensuring
all the steam escapes.

Celadon

I never stop to think if there are others like me,
cupping the newfound weight of themselves and discovering

more than they'd thought possible. I remember being
told the name of a place that seemed impossible to reach,

but I'm sure I visited once, when I was younger,
too overwhelmed to have named it.

✳

A steady feeling of excess, of something pulling.

✳

I spend a deal of time searching for clues.

Celadon – don't you see how it is both hard and soft?

The closest match is *epididymal cyst*. This is a temporary name.

✳

Something without a face is approaching.

I'm taken out of school for an entire day!

We're heading to *Leicester*, a jumbling of letters.
Lucy eats ice cream every Saturday teatime except on rainy days.

Lucy can be *Lurgy*, or *Lump*, or *Lull*.

＊

I'm remembering more of the city – when I visited,
everything was green and filled with flowers.
A man with nowhere to be was peering intently
through a frosted glass window.

The room is painted for children.

I'm developing a fascination
with *celadon*. It rolls around my mouth
like a marble. Every time I'm reminded of it
it feels like I'm standing at a great height.

＊

As the day stretches, a stubborn tree springs back to life
and must be cut down. This happens very often.
The second time I visit everything is more vibrant, detailed.

It's extremely easy to pretend everything
is fine, that everything is still
how it used to be. The city roughly maintains

its shape – though one house has moved
an entire eleven feet to the right,
and I'm exactly two inches taller.

＊

A woman is waiting, standing on artificial grass.
She's repeating a complex phrase under her breath.

A man talks of my body with indifference. He gestures
with his blue-green hands. I'm not sure if there's a word

for impossible place. How strange to talk about it
as if it belongs to me.

To see yourself twice is a great gift.

Whatever Happened to Billy Hatcher

you let yourself into my coop
and call me Hen Mother   leave
scratch-marks and droppings
on my floor and tell me that you
work miracles   you help me feel

true morning   your song can
stir creatures still waiting to be
born   when the foxes come
you cannot stop weeping   oh Billy
in some lights you resemble

the rooster   your snapped neck
grants me just one wish   how
easily you get up to leave when
I give you my egg   why don't you
sing to it Billy   why don't you sing

The Most Kissed Face of All Time

Resusci Anne's incorporation of life-like facial features helped increase the realism of resuscitation training, making CPR training more intense and stressful for both clinicians and lay-people – but also more memorable as a result, which aids recall of the technique.

We knelt around the dead girl, listening. She made no sound yet the room was never silent. It all seemed so complex – the steps to take, the exactness of it. The instructor circled us, arms behind her back. *You must make sure the area is safe. You must prioritise yourselves.* We feigned checking for hazards, wet floors, exposed wires, unsure of how we'd prepare for actual dangers, unsure of what we'd really do.

We leaned over the dead girl to check if she was breathing. When we noticed she wasn't, one of us began phoning for help, another went searching for a defibrillator. I pushed down on her chest and it clicked, over and over. The instructor warned us we would most likely break something, somewhere, but that it would be worth it if it meant saving a life. I believed her. She'd told us stories of men collapsing on stairs, of dislocated shoulders, of doing nothing but waiting. She told me to kiss the dead girl and I did, forced air in, felt her chest rise. I wondered if there were other ways of saving lives but I couldn't think of any because I'd only been taught one. The dead girl stayed dead, mouth open, waiting to be cleaned.

Plateau–Rayleigh Instability

that long summer when we were kids
inventing fun between sisters

me parading like a good little sister
perfectly in character   you watching

in silence   your thundercloud face

humming before glowing before cracking

I was trying so hard   to impress you

and willing to perform   becoming air

climbing the stairs   like you told me to

you at the bottom   arms out   saying

go on   go on

the flat top of the landing   me somersaulting

the plateau   (you)   disappearing

me   of course   falling   like   rain

Kitty

she slips past   reduces   becomes air
in the state where she is less than solid

Kitty falls straight through her bed   lands
an entire floor below in her sister's old room

finds so many forgotten clothes   all lilac
reminding her of the hard stone   bruised chin
impact at the foot of the stairs   her sister

somewhere nearby yet distant   the hall
becoming unfathomable   its state shifting

panic   the shoe caught in the bottom step
how did it hold itself there so easily   rigid

and suspended   her sister shouting   how
did you do that   where are you going   Kitty
you're disappearing   Kitty don't go

today down the street all the shopkeepers
close their blinds as if it might deter Kitty

not that she cares   she can only think
of not falling   she grows exhausted

as the sun sets   stumbles right into
a townhouse   new build   not yet lived in
finds her sister hunched over   older

struggling to tie her stubborn shoelaces
and grieving their mother   furiously

chanting under her breath but
it passes straight through   Kitty

tries to help like any sister would

but she can't hold anything up

Sister leaves home during our favourite show

You told me you were leaving while we were watching TV, the screen arguing with itself, bleaching the shadows in the room turquoise. I was staring hard at your shoulders as you forced your life into a backpack too small. We'd been watching a repeat of our favourite show, making our way through season two, waiting for our favourite character. We knew which scene came next: the acrobat, the martial artist, the best friend. We knew how fast she would move between people, how precise she'd be, striking the most tender parts of each body, how quickly they'd give up and soften at her touch.

You were folding clothes when she appeared and when I tried to stop you, filling the space between us with my clumsiness, hoping each hit might hold a part of you back. You didn't flinch but you were hurting in some unusual way, and then you and your bag were gone, leaving me rolling my wrist and resenting the acrobat, how she could be so impossibly exact, how I already knew how the season ended, but still let the TV play on.

But This Was Never About the Swimmers

I am followed by an unshakable feeling
that I should have noticed your hands

hesitating when you unhooked the ropes
at the pool   rolled everything in   how typical

of them   heavy with water   to fall from
the rusted wheel   and you without a word

unwinding and starting the process all over
how typical of those lonely swimmers

who think if they push their bodies
between the roped-off lanes   they might

just once   be surprised at what can happen
when we go beyond what we think we can do

after their aching muscles have finished
sobbing   at the side   drawing in great breaths

and you   hunched over   head between
your knees   wondering how many times

would you have to to loop the ropes back
before everything was in its place

Now That We Receive Regular Updates the Glitches Have Been Resolved

it wasn't so much the thrill of falling through something solid
but rather the potential to find accidental places

the anticipation / unknown / fluke

standing beneath a giant rock

        slipping through a loosely-meshed corner

a shortcut

the idea of making some form of progress but absolutely unexpectedly

deciding what could be claimed / breaking the rules

      climbing dangerously high

discovering never finished / never worked-on spaces

        becoming non-linear

the day after I tried so many times to get back
I tried jumping I tried crouching I tried all I could
but nothing worked they fixed it they fixed everything

Canary Song

the first time I cry / I feel more like my sister than ever / she
had a way of seeing / the best in people / sometimes I must
wear a mask and sometimes I must not / I have never tried
to be anything / more than my sister / I have known the feeling
of losing her more than once / my sweet forgotten

sister / when she returned I was still so young / it is easy to not
remember / I have friends who might miss me / four years after
my sister died I told the man I loved I still loved him / sometimes
it is hard to tell / the difference between crying and singing / I will
never sing like my sister / my sister was a canary / oh how she sang

Practice

I am playing Victim again

        waiting to be rolled over and dragged

to safety   it is difficult to fake drowning

        when you can swim   I am trying my best

to be as heavy as I can   I try telling Rescuer this

        but Rescuer has one chlorine-rough hand on my chin

and I cannot speak   Rescuer's knees are pressing

        into my back   I go limp and let myself be

rocked with the motions of Rescuer's kicking

        it is easiest to do nothing and wait for Rescuer

to reach the side   Rescuer holds me up

        against the lip   Rescuer is practising

technique on how to save Victim

        I am practising how I would be Victim

or better practising how I would wait to be saved

        it is like learning to be very soft

Acknowledgements

Versions of some of the poems in this pamphlet have previously appeared in the following publications: *In the Red*; *Orris Root*; *Magma*; *The North*.

I'm extremely grateful to everyone who's read and re-read my poems over the past few years: Gregory Kearns, Megan Bagnall, Andrew McMillan, Helen Tookey; to everyone on my MA course who shared their valuable insights; to everyone at Bluecoat, to Mary Jean Chan, Suzannah Evans, Katie McLean, and all at The Poetry Business, for without their support this would have never happened; to Mom and Dad, who (mostly) always said yes.